GRACE TO GO ON

GRACE TO GO ON

VICTOR BOOKS®

A DIVISION OF SCRIPTURE PRESS PUBLICATIONS INC.
USA CANADA ENGLAND

4 5 6 7 8 9 10 Printing/Year 94 93

Recommended Dewey Decimal Classification: 231.3
Suggested Subject Heading: HOLY SPIRIT

Library of Congress Catalog Card Number: 89-60175
ISBN: 0-89693-762-3

VICTOR BOOKS
A division of SP Publications, Inc.
       Wheaton, Illinois 60187

•CONTENTS•

*Recognition to Beth Donigan Seversen
for assistance
in researching and formulating
parts of this book.*

•INTRODUCTION•

The Holy Spirit gives us "grace to go on" to maturity. He sustains and encourages us, gifts and enables us. He grows the fruit of Christian character in our lives and teaches us God's truth. Symbols of the Spirit abound in Scripture. Studying them, we can come to an experience of the Spirit that will enrich our souls.

SYMBOLS

the *fire* ignites
the *wind* of change
the *oil* of gladness
the *water* of life
the abused *dove*
the Spirit's *gifts*
the *fruit* that blossoms
the *cloud* of Glory

•BEFORE YOU BEGIN•

People who gather together for Bible study are likely to be at different places in their spiritual lives, and their study materials should be flexible enough to meet their different needs. This book is designed to be used as a Bible study guide for such groups in homes or churches. It can also be used by individuals who are studying on their own. The lessons are written in five distinct sections, so that they can be used in a variety of situations. Groups and individuals alike can choose to use the elements they find most useful in the order they find most beneficial.

These studies will help you learn some new truths from the Bible as well as how to dig out those truths. You will learn not only *what* the Bible says, but how to use Scripture to deepen your relationship with Jesus Christ by obeying it and applying it in daily living. These studies will also provide an opportunity for potential leaders to learn how to lead a discussion in a nonthreatening setting.

What You'll Need
For each study you will need a Bible and this Bible study guide. You might also want to have a notebook in which to record your thoughts and discoveries from your personal study and group meetings. A notebook could also be used to record prayer requests from the group.

The Sections
Food for Thought. This is a devotional narrative that introduces the topic, person, or passage featured in the lesson. There are several ways it can be used. Each person could read it before coming to the group meeting, and someone could briefly summarize it at the beginning. It could be read silently by each person at the beginning of the session, or it could be read aloud, by one or several group members. (Suggested time: 10 minutes)

Talking It Over. This section contains discussion questions to help you review what you learned in Food for Thought. There are also questions to help you apply the narrative's truths to daily life. The person who leads the discussion of these questions need not be a trained or experienced teacher. All that is needed is someone to keep things moving and facilitate group interaction. (Suggested time: 30 minutes)

Praying It Through. This is a list of suggestions for prayer based on the lesson. You may want to use all the suggestions or eliminate some in order to leave more time for personal sharing and prayer requests. (Suggested time: 20 minutes)

Digging Deeper. The questions in this section are also related to the passage, topic, or character from the lesson. But they will not always be limited to the exact passage or character from Food for Thought. Passages and characters from both the Old and New Testaments will appear in this section, in order to show how God has worked through *all* of history in people's lives. These questions will require a little more thinking and some digging into Scripture, as well as some use of Bible study tools. Participants will be stretched as they become experienced in the "how-tos" of Bible study. (Suggested time: 45 minutes)

8

Tool Chest. The Tool Chest contains a description of a specific type of Bible study help and includes an explanation of how it is used. An example of the tool is given, and an example of it or excerpt from it is usually included in the Digging Deeper study.

The Bible study helps in the Tool Chest can be purchased by anyone who desires to build a basic library of Bible study reference books and other tools. They would also be good additions to a church library. Some are reasonably inexpensive, but others are quite expensive. A few may be available in your local library or in a seminary or college library. A group might decide to purchase one tool during each series and build a corporate tool chest for all the members of the group to use. You can never be too young a Christian to begin to master Bible study helps, nor can you be too old to learn new methods of rightly dividing the Word of truth.

Options for Group Use
Different groups, made up of people at diverse stages of spiritual growth, will want to use the elements in this book in different ways. Here are a few suggestions to get you started, but be creative and sensitive to your group's needs.

☐ Spend 5-15 minutes at the beginning of the group time introducing yourselves and having group members answer an icebreaker question. (Sample icebreaker questions are included under Tips for Leaders.)

☐ Extend the prayer time to include sharing of prayer requests, praise items, or things group members have learned recently in their times of personal Bible study.

☐ The leader could choose questions for discussion from the Digging Deeper section based on whether participants have prepared ahead of time or not.

☐ The entire group could break into smaller groups to allow different groups to use different sections. (The smaller groups could move to other rooms in the home or church where you are meeting.)

Tips for Leaders
Preparation
1. Pray for the Holy Spirit's guidance as you study, that you will be equipped to teach the lesson and make it appealing and applicable.
2. Read through the entire lesson and any Bible passages or verses that are mentioned. Answer all the questions.
3. Become familiar enough with the lesson that, if time in the

group is running out, you know which questions could most easily be left out.

4. Gather all the items you will need for the study: name tags, extra pens, extra Bibles.

The Meeting
1. Start and end on time.
2. Have everyone wear a name tag until group members know one another's names.
3. Have each person introduce himself or herself, or ask regular attenders to introduce guests.
4. For each meeting, pick an icebreaker question or another activity to help group members get to know one another better.
5. Use any good ideas to make everyone feel comfortable.

The Discussion
1. Ask the questions, but try to let the group answer. Don't be afraid of silence. Reword the question if it is unclear to the group or answer it yourself to clarify.
2. Encourage everyone to participate. If someone is shy, ask that person to answer an opinion question or another nonthreatening question. If someone tends to monopolize the discussion, thank that person for his or her contribution and ask if someone else has anything he or she would like to add. (Or ask that person to make the coffee!)
3. If someone gives an incorrect answer, don't bluntly or tactlessly tell him or her so. If it is partly right, reinforce that. Ask if anyone else has any thoughts on the subject. (Disagree agreeably!)
4. Avoid tangents. If someone is getting off the subject, ask that person how his or her point relates to the lesson.
5. Don't feel threatened if someone asks a question you can't answer. Tell the person you don't know but will find out before the next meeting—then be sure to find out! Or ask if someone would like to research and present the answer at the group's next meeting.

Icebreaker Questions
The purpose of these icebreaker questions is to help the people in your group get to know one another over the course of the study. The questions you use when your group members don't know one another very well should be very general and nonthreatening. As time goes on, your questions can become more focused and specific.

Always give group members the option of passing if they think a question is too personal.

What do you like to do for fun?
What is your favorite season? dessert? book?
What would be your ideal vacation?
What exciting thing happened to you this week?
What was the most memorable thing you did with your family when you were a child?
What one word best describes the way you feel today?
Tell three things you are thankful for.
Imagine that your house is on fire. What three things would you try to take with you on your way out?
If you were granted one wish, what would it be?
What experience of your past would you most enjoy reliving?
What quality do you most appreciate in a friend?
What is your pet peeve?
What is something you are learning to do or trying to get better at?
What is your greatest hope?
What is your greatest fear?
What one thing would you like to change about yourself?
What has been the greatest accomplishment of your life?
What has been the greatest disappointment of your life?

Need More Help?
Here is a list of books that contain helpful information on leading discussions and working in groups:

> *How to Lead Small Group Bible Studies* (NavPress, 1982).
> *Creative Bible Learning for Adults,* Monroe Marlowe and Bobbie Reed (Regal, 1977).
> *Getting Together,* Em Griffin (InterVarsity Press, 1982).
> *Good Things Come in Small Groups* (InterVarsity Press, 1985).

One Last Thought
This book is a tool you can use whether you have one or one hundred people who want to study the Bible and whether you have one or no teachers. Don't wait for a brilliant Bible study leader to appear—most such teachers acquired their skills by starting with a book like this and learning as they went along. Torrey said, "The best way to begin, is to begin." Happy beginnings!

1
Fire

•FOOD FOR THOUGHT•

A headline focuses our attention and captures the news for us. Tabloids and newspapers know that. That's why a glance through a news magazine gives us a feel for a prevailing sentiment, a political trend, the pulse of our world. Last time I read some of these headlines, I gathered we were in big trouble—all of us! Those who share this planet of problems with us were saying it's tough being a human being these days. From the heat of Yellowstone's charcoal to the young escapee on the Berlin wall screaming out in terror at the guards—"don't shoot, I have a baby in my stomach"—to the hunger fields where starving people fight to get a chicken head to eat, our world cries out, "time out, this can't be real, it has to be a nightmare!" But for many people the bad dream has already come true. The IRA bomb explodes leaving one legged people balancing the rest of their lives on a crutch, watching their children with one eye. Couples try to invent new sophisticated methods to pick and claw each other's emotions to shreds. Whatever happened to Eden?

Across the pain, here and there a voice is heard, using its bow of belief to play a tune of truth on an instrument that has been playing sad songs. The voice says—"Christ and His cross are the answer—there *is* grace to go on!" The Spirit of grace grows faith in the faithless, hope in the hopeless, love in the loveless, joy in the joyless, depth in the shallow one, care in the cruel one, even a big man inside a little man! There is grace to go on and grow on—both—because the Spirit of grace is come!

One particular magazine I was reading led me down a dark tunnel of despair until right at the end I discovered a tune of truth! I found myself looking at this lovely, refined-looking lady (English, of course), Cecily Saunders. For over two years she has helped 13,000 people to die with dignity. Sustained by her evangelical belief, this

70-year-old founder of the modern hospice movement has helped frightened people who were very ill know that though "death is an outrage for those left behind"—it isn't the end (*Time*). For the Christian, parting at death isn't forever. There's not only grace to go on for the dying, but also grace to stop going on! Cecily Saunders believes there is "grace to help in time of need." The agent of this given grace is the third person of the Trinity—the Holy Spirit. Of course, the Holy Spirit isn't only there for the dying, but for the living too! He it is with whom we have to do. And yet so few of us have anything to do with Him! This is because believers harbor so many misconceptions about His identity.

When I first came to America I had many misconceptions about lots of things. For example, I believed you could go right through the day without eating a chocolate chip cookie! I was soon put right about that as a friend arrived with a mixing bowl and ingredients to help me learn to make the essential American dainties! God would deal with far more serious misconceptions for those of us who count ourselves evangelical believers. He wants to correct wrong thinking about the Holy Spirit's work.

What are some of these wrong ideas? The first one is that the Holy Spirit's importance is minimal. J. Oswald Sanders quotes A.W. Tozer on this point: "In most Christian churches the Spirit is entirely overlooked. Whether He is present or absent makes no real difference to anyone. Brief reference is made to Him in the Doxology and the Benediction. Further than that, He might as well not exist. So completely do we ignore Him that it is only by courtesy that we can be called Trinitarian. . . . The idea of the Spirit held by the average church member is so vague as to be nearly non-existent" (*The Holy Spirit and His Gifts*, Zondervan, p. 10). David Watson, an Anglican minister from England, accused evangelicals of worshiping God, Christ, and the Holy Scriptures—rather than the Holy Spirit.

Sins of ignorance, however, are one thing (and something we hope to redress by this study). But sins of apathy concerning these matters are quite another! Apathy can include the sin of willful blindness. It is the opposite of *gnosis* or knowledge which is an opportunity to learn as a result of observation and experience. This is no unwitting error and very serious in matters concerning God. Knowledge comes as a result of observation and experience "helped" by the Holy Spirit. In John 14:15-20 we are told that He is the Spirit of truth and a teacher of that truth par excellence.

He is also called the *paraclete*. This means He is an advocate with God. Jesus encouraged the disciples to take hope by looking forward to His coming. Even though He was leaving them, He promised to send them another Counselor. The word *another* describes Him as another being of exactly the same sort as Himself.

"You know Him," the Lord explained to the disciples, "for He lives with you and will be in you" (v. 17). The word *counselor* or *paraclete* is a legal term and refers to someone who helps anyone in trouble with the law. The idea is that He is "one called alongside to help." He is a Helper. The Holy Spirit, however, is more than a counsel for the defense. He is no heavenly Perry Mason, though He has been called the Divine Barrister. He is, after all, the third person of the Trinity!

The root significance of the word *counselor* is strength and power. The idea of comfort or counsel is secondary and rather dilutes the full meaning of the nature of the word. The element of comfort is an important aspect of His work and Jesus uses the picture of comforting the desolate as one comforts an orphan, but the primary thought for us must be that of advocate. An advocate is one who is called to one's side for help especially against an accuser or judge. He is the client's representative who pleads his case and defends his reputation, guarding and administrating his property.

Oswald Sanders says the Holy Spirit is not our advocate, but rather Christ's! The Son is our advocate with the Father (1 John 1:2), while the Spirit is the advocate of the Son on earth. Catherine Marshall lights up this thought by saying that Christ is in the spotlight that is held by the Holy Spirit (*The Helper*). Therefore, it follows that the Holy Spirit will involve us in His work of looking after Jesus Christ's interests, focusing the world's attention upon Him.

As He is God Omnipotent, so He is Omniscient too. He is the Spirit of truth. Jesus has just been telling the disciples the Spirit knows what God has prepared for us (John 14:1-4). He knows because He knows the very thoughts of God and the mind of Christ (1 Corinthians 2:9-16). If He knows so much, then it's easy to grasp the fact He wants to share this knowledge with us!

Because He is God, He is also Omnipresent. When Christ lived among men, He limited Himself to a Galilean frame. He could not be in Jerusalem and Bethlehem at one and the same time. However, Jesus promised that when the Holy Spirit came, He would be unlimited. The Holy Spirit would be Omnipresent, speaking to the African bush man, the Australian executive, the English lady, the Asian street sweeper—all at the same moment of "man time."

Remember that when Jesus spoke to His disciples about the Holy Spirit, He was trying to comfort them. He had just broken the news that He was going to leave them. He said that His departure would actually be to their advantage and that in the future at any given moment of time, He would be with them all wherever they all would be. He would "never leave them or forsake any of them" (Hebrews 13:5). And this was not to be for their sakes alone. The Holy Spirit's work was to be Christ's Advocate, looking after His interests. This would bring conflict as the forces of evil rallied against God's people and His cause.

After all, the Holy Spirit's job would be to convict the world of sin—or expose the guilt of the world (John 16). What guilt? The guilt of their unbelief! Apart from the work of the Holy Spirit, people do not see themselves as sinners. Unbelief in Jesus Christ is sin, and the Spirit will convince people of that! The Spirit's work means that man will begin to take sin—that sin, very seriously indeed. But not only would the Holy Spirit convict the world of sin, He would convert the world to Christ! And once converted, He would comfort and console those who had been so convinced and converted!

Jesus told His disciples there was a divine agenda concerning the Holy Spirit. According to prophecy He would come "in the last days" (Joel 2:29) and according to Jesus He would come only after He had "gone away." In other words, the Holy Spirit would be given after the Cross and Resurrection. In Acts 2:1-13, we read about Pentecost and how the Holy Spirit was poured out upon the waiting disciples in the Upper Room.

"They saw what seemed to be tongues of fire" hovering over each one present (Acts 2:3). The fire was not "real" fire but was an emblem or symbol. When we hear that the Holy Spirit is like fire, it helps us to understand His nature. Fire is one of the mightiest and most terrible forces known to man, and represents the presence of the Triune God. The Spirit Himself is called "the Spirit of burning" (Isaiah 33:14). The burning zeal that would turn the world upside down (or rather right side up) would purify the dross in men's lives, leaving their gold faith shining brightly.

Do you know by personal experience the presence, power, and purifying work of the Holy Spirit in your life?

•TALKING IT OVER•

1. DISCUSS.
   5 *minutes*
   ☐ Is the doctrine of the Holy Spirit taught in our churches today? Why, or why not?

2. REVIEW JOHN 14:15-20.
   10 *minutes*
   Which verses teach us about our
   ☐ Advocate
   ☐ Teacher
   ☐ Comforter
   Think of the Holy Spirit as our "Divine Barrister." Is this a helpful picture? Why?
   Review John 16:5-16. Choose a verse you like and say why.

3. DISCUSS THE SYMBOL OF FIRE.
   5 *minutes*
   ☐ Circle the picture that helped you most.
   fire burns   fire glows   fire purifies

•PRAYING IT THROUGH•

Suggested Times

---

1. (As a group) Read John 14:15, 20 and mix these words with your own to have a time of praise.

5 minutes

---

2. (As a group) Pray for:
   □ The conviction of sin in nonbelievers' hearts.
   □ The convincing work of the Holy Spirit as He points to Christ. Particularly remember cults, work among Muslims, and churchgoers who reject the deity of Christ.
   □ The conversion of family members.

10 minutes

---

3. (In twos) Pray for the "Pentecost" you personally need in terms of a sense of His presence, power, or purity.

5 minutes

•DIGGING DEEPER•

The Spirit and the Old Testament

In the Digging Deeper sections we will systematically be studying the Spirit as He is mentioned in the Scriptures. Our aim will be to learn what the Bible itself has to say about the person and work of the Spirit.

Each Scripture emphasizes His various characteristics. From these passages, try to describe the Spirit's roles and activities and answer the corresponding questions. Make certain you read the context surrounding each verse.

1. Read the following Scriptures and determine what work(s) is attributed to the Spirit.

   Genesis 1:2

   Job 33:4

   Psalm 104:24-30

   How does this correlate with other Scripture relating to the subject?

   Isaiah 45:11-12, 18

   Jeremiah 10:16

   John 1:3

   Colossians 1:16

2. The Old Testament writers often employed parallelism as a literary technique. This is a poetic form where a second line

repeats, contrasts, or elaborates upon the idea presented in the first line for the purpose of emphasis. What do each of the following parallel constructions indicate about the Spirit?

Psalm 51:11

Psalm 139:7

With what or whom is the Spirit equated?

3. What is unusual about the characteristics the Spirit is displaying in the following passages?

Isaiah 11:2

Isaiah 63:10

Micah 2:7

Psalm 106:33

This affirms that the Spirit is not what?

4. The Spirit empowered the men in the following passages for what specific tasks?

Exodus 31:1-5

Zechariah 4

What does this teach about the Spirit's ministry?

5. Read the following passages and note how the Spirit operated in the lives of the leaders. How did He equip them? What did He enable them to do?

Numbers 11:16-17

Numbers 27:18-23

Deuteronomy 34:9

Judges 3:10

Judges 6:34

Judges 11:29-33

Judges 13:25

Judges 14:5-6, 19

Judges 15:14-15

6. Read the following verses and determine what the Spirit empowered Saul for.

   1 Samuel 10:6

   1 Samuel 11:6-8

   1 Samuel 16:13-14

   What do these incidents reveal about the Spirit's endowment during Old Testament times?

7. Describe what can be determined of the Spirit's function in prophecy.

   2 Peter 1:21

   Numbers 24:1-2, 10-13

   1 Samuel 19:14-24

   2 Samuel 23:2

   2 Chronicles 20:14

2 Chronicles 24:20

Nehemiah 9:30

Isaiah 61:1

Ezekiel 11:5ff

Joel 2:28

Zechariah 7:12

Micah 3:8

What did the prophets understand to be the Spirit's role in their ministries?

8. Study these passages in Isaiah to see what effect the Spirit was to have on the Messiah.

Isaiah 11:1-3

Isaiah 42:1

Isaiah 61:1 (cf. Luke 4:16-21)

9. Explain the Spirit's expected activity in the future restoration of Israel as described in each passage.

Isaiah 59:21

Ezekiel 36:27

Joel 2:28

10. Write a brief report of what you have learned from the Old Testament regarding the Spirit's person and work. You may wish to use additional paper.

11. Would you like the Spirit to act in your life in a similar fashion to His actions in Old Testament times? If so, how? What ministry, practical or spiritual, do you desire the Spirit to equip and enable you for? How would you like to see His power evidenced in your life?

For Further Study
  1. Using a concordance, make a list of all the Old Testament names or descriptions of the Spirit. What do these add to your understanding of Him?
  2. Review your study and ask yourself if the Spirit operates today in similar ways as He did in ancient times. If so, answer in what ways and support your premise. If not, why not and how does He function differently?

• TOOL CHEST •
(A Suggested Optional Resource)

BIBLICAL INTERPRETATION TOOLS
Have you sometimes wondered if you may be guilty of quoting a verse out of context, spiritualizing a text, or being untrue to the intended meaning of a biblical passage? *How To Read the Bible for All It's Worth* (Zondervan), by Gordan Fee and Douglas Stuart, can help you learn how to apply the necessary principles of interpretation to your Bible study. This tool serves as a practical resource guide for correctly determining the meaning of parables as well as apocalyptic and prophetic literature. Many make the easy mistake of skipping from observation to application without adequately interpreting the Scriptures. Books on interpretation and hermeneutics can prevent this error and assist the reader's understanding of difficult or obscure texts. More sources on this subject include:

Hermeneutics by Henry A. Virkler (Baker)
How To Understand Your Bible by T. Norton Sterrett (InterVarsity)
Interpreting the Bible by A. Berkeley Mickelsen (Eerdmans)
A Layman's Guide to Studying the Bible by Walter A. Henrichsen (Zondervan)

2
Wind

•FOOD FOR THOUGHT•

Oswald Sanders said: "It is a principle of Scripture that the names and emblems by which God has chosen to reveal Himself are intended to give insight into His true nature" (*The Holy Spirit and His Gifts*, Zondervan, p. 30). His basic name *Spirit* or *Spiritus* is the Latin synonym for the Greek word *pneuma*. The Hebrew word *ruach* carries the same idea. Both significantly speak of breath, wind, or air. In John 3:8 Jesus tells Nicodemus that the Holy Spirit is like the wind. The picture helps us to realize one more aspect of the Spirit's nature.

First of all, the Spirit is like a gentle breeze! He, the Holy Spirit, is the out-breathing of God. He is His direct emanation imparting His quickening life. In creation "the Lord God formed the man from the dust of the ground and breathed into his nostrils the breath of life, and the man became a living being" (Genesis 2:7). Someone has said the breath of life and the Holy Spirit hold hands—they go together. Numbers 16:22 tells us that God is "God of the spirits of all mankind." The Lord God gives life to man's body—a life shared by the animals.

But God not only gave life to our bodies—causing blood to flow through our veins, the heart to beat rhythmically, and the cells of the skin to begin to renew themselves daily—He gave life to the Spirit of man also. Man became a living being not merely a living body. He was then able to respond to God in a unique way. I love to picture the Holy Spirit as a gentle breeze. It brings to mind the Divine Potter forming man and gently blowing the breath of life into the sticky wet work—"and man became a living soul!"

But then sin entered the universe, God inhaled His breath in horror and sorrow, and man died. The Holy Spirit was "gone." The body and soul, however, took a little longer to pass away. Man was

26

physically alive but spiritually dead. He was on dry land like a fish gasping for breath; it was only a matter of time. In the Old Testament, the Holy Spirit breathed into one soul here and there bringing spiritual life. The Spirit stayed if the person maintained a life of obedience and holiness. If the person rebelled, however, the Holy Spirit withdrew.

In the New Testament, Jesus gave the Spirit to His disciples to help them accomplish their work. "Jesus breathed on them and said receive ye the Holy Spirit" (John 20:22). But it wasn't until the day of Pentecost the gentle life-giving breath of the Spirit of God became like a strong wind blowing on all believing men and women indiscriminately, in a way He had never been bestowed before! The sound of that mysterious supernatural wind could be heard from all quarters of Jerusalem and instituted a change that was to leave the whole world standing on its head.

The symbolic picture of a mysterious wind coming from the four corners of the earth in renewing force is seen in Ezekiel 37. The prophet has a vision of a valley filled with dry bones. He is told they represent the whole house of Israel. "Preach to them!" God says! Used to preaching to people not bones, Ezekiel hesitates but then obeys. As the Word of God is received the sinews, flesh, and skin grow on the pile of dry desolate dislocated bones and the prophet sees a cavern full of corpses instead of a valley full of bones! Instead of a cemetery, Ezekiel is now faced with a mortuary! Both are as tragic as each other of course. It makes little difference if the whole house of Israel is a heap of bones or a pile of corpses—both need life!

Next the prophet hears the Lord God telling him to pray to the wind and call to the breath of God, to come from the four corners of the earth to revive the dead men. God answers the prophet's prayer, the wind of the Spirit comes, and life enters into the corpses producing "a vast army" (Ezekiel 37:10).

In John 3, we are told that Nicodemus, a prominent pharisee, came to Jesus by night. Nicodemus lived in a cemetery called the nation of Israel. His job had been to preach to the dry bones. Jesus calls him "Israel's teacher" (John 3:10). Nicodemus' problem surpassed Ezekiel's problem however, as he himself was a dry bone and had no spiritual life in him at all. He knew that the synagogue was full of spiritual skeletons though and was concerned about it. Somehow, he believed Jesus had some answers for him. Jesus confirmed his belief and urged him to get personally involved with the Spirit of life. In effect, Jesus first challenged Nicodemus to pray to the wind.

Then he gave him a message to take away to preach to the bones!

Jesus used the same symbol to explain the Holy Spirit's work as Ezekiel had—the wind. He explained to Nicodemus that he needed to be born from above (John 3:3-8). Nicodemus had been born physically with the gentle breath of God giving life to his flesh. But there was something more. Now the teacher of Israel needed to be born spiritually. The vivifying life of the Spirit needed to bring life to Nicodemus' spirit, which in a way was even a greater miracle than that of his physical birth.

Jesus made it a very personal thing to Nicodemus in John 3:7 when he said, "You" (John 3:7). Then He made it sound quite essential—"must." He showed how "eternal" a matter it was, explaining that life in the kingdom of God could not even begin without the activity of the Holy Spirit. He explained that Nicodemus must be related to Him by being "born again" and that this could only be brought about by the work of the Holy Spirit. Using another picture—that of the Israelites bitten by snakes who looked to the serpent set up by Moses on a pole in the middle of the camp—Jesus challenged Nicodemus to look to Him and live.

Jesus points out that the wind is a mysterious thing. "You cannot tell where it comes from or where it is going" (John 3:8). But He might have added we can surely tell just where it has been. In other words the effects of the wind's presence will be evidenced! Let's stop a moment and ask a question. Have we received physical life? Well that's easy; we wouldn't be reading this if we hadn't! Have we received spiritual life? That's harder for some of us to answer. Then let us consider whether the wind has changed us or if our lives look just the same today as ever.

The last picture of the wind of God is given to us in Acts 2. This time it is not a gentle breath or even a moderate wind, but rather a mighty blast. The church is born! The Bible says it happened with a sound like the "blowing of a violent wind" (Acts 2:2). The Spirit flooded the upper room and the people in it and the sound seemed to fill Jerusalem. This was a wind that was heard but not felt. An entirely supernatural sound!

The mighty wind spoke of the very presence of God. This wind had been heard before when Ezekiel had his vision by the Kebar River (Ezekiel 3:12). Then the prophet had heard a loud rushing, rumbling and rattling—like a mighty wind as he saw the wondrous spirit beings.

Pentecost left no one asleep in the heat of the day! The wind excited the disciples, invited attention, incited response, and ignited

3,000 people! The disciples now discovered they had power to preach, power to be different, and power to work together in unity. Like a hurricane the arrival of the Holy Spirit was somewhat difficult to ignore!

So the gentle breeze of God's Spirit brings life to our body while the mysterious wind gives life to our soul. The mighty blast that Joel promised sweeps us up into the purposes of God for our lives and lends us power to be different to do exploits, and to bring glory to God. We can do none of these things in our own energy. This is the work of the Holy Spirit.

May God bend us to the winds of His will!

•TALKING IT OVER•

1. REVIEW.
   Which picture caught your attention and why?
   □ The gentle breeze
   □ The mysterious wind
   □ The hurricane

   7 minutes

2. READ AND DISCUSS.
   Read Ezekiel 33 and John 3:8. The wind is featured in both Scriptures.
   □ What similarities can you find?
   □ What differences? Discuss.

   15 minutes

3. READ.
   Read Joel 2.
   □ When will the Spirit be given?
   □ Who will be the recipients?
   □ Can we expect the power of Pentecost in our lives today?

   8 minutes

•PRAYING IT THROUGH•

Suggested Times

1. (On your own) Pray for people you know who are like Nicodemus. Pray for others who need to be *born again*. Pray they will realize that the experience of being born again is:
☐ Personal
☐ Essential
☐ Eternal

8 minutes

2. (As a group) Read John 3:16 and praise Him for all the information you find there. Then read John 3:36 and pray for those you love who are in eternal danger.

8 minutes

3. (As a group) Pray for your leaders, that they will know Pentecostal power. Pray they will know a boldness and effectiveness in their ministry. Use the words of the hymn "Breathe on Me Breath of God" as a prayer to finish.

4 minutes

•DIGGING DEEPER•

The Spirit and the Synoptic Gospels

The term synoptic refers to giving a summary or an explanation from a similar viewpoint. Matthew, Mark, and Luke are called the synoptic gospels because their summaries of the life, person, and work of Jesus Christ follow similar formats and present much of the same material.

1. Luke records the Spirit's involvement in the birth of John the Baptist. Read the following Scriptures and describe the Spirit's activity in each account. Note the context and answer the subsequent questions.

   Luke 1:15

   Luke 1:41

   Luke 1:67

   When and how was John filled with the Spirit?

   In what ways was his filling similar or dissimilar to the filling of the Old Testament prophets?

   What is the stated link between John and the prophets?

From what you know of the prophets' ministry, what might this hint about John's future ministry?

With regard to the Messiah, what was John's mission? Why would he need the Spirit's filling for these tasks?

How did the Holy Spirit prompt or inspire Elizabeth?

2. The following passages recount the birth of Christ Jesus. Explain the Spirit's role in the incarnation and birth narratives.

Matthew 1:18

Matthew 1:20

Luke 1:35

Luke 2:25

Luke 2:26

Luke 2:27

Explain the Spirit's role in Mary's conception. How many times is this stated?

3. Luke is careful to point out that the Holy Spirit was upon Simeon (v. 25). Why? What does the Spirit reveal to Simeon? What importance does this incident have?

The Spirit is a critical part of John's message and Jesus' baptism. Examine these verses to answer the following questions: Matthew 3:1-12; Mark 1:8; Luke 3:1-9, 15-17.

How does John distinguish his ministry and baptism from Christ's ministry and baptism?

What does fire signify, and why would it be linked to the Holy Spirit? (Matthew 3:11; Luke 3:16)

After you have examined the contexts you may wish to consult a reference help. In Pastor John Mackett's class notes on the Holy Spirit, he indicates fire may refer to the judgment to come on those who do not repent, or it may refer to purgation, the act of being rid of impurities such as sin or guilt (used by permission).

Why does John consider his baptism to be inferior to Christ's?

4. Did the baptism Jesus was to do have anything to do with water? What did it have to do with? (cf. Matthew 3:13-17; Mark 1:9-11; Luke 3:21-22)

Explain Jesus' reason for insisting on being baptized by John.

Why do you think the Spirit is mentioned as present at Jesus' baptism in all three accounts? What would His appearance signify?

How is the Spirit compared to a dove?

5. After Jesus' baptism, it is mentioned that He is immediately led by the Spirit into the desert where He is tempted by Satan for a period of time. Study this event in the following passages:

Matthew 4:1-11

Mark 1:12-13

Luke 4:1-13

How did the Spirit participate in Jesus' temptation? What part might He have played in Jesus' resistance to the devil from what you learned about Him in your Old Testament study?

6. Read Luke 11:1-13. What instructions did Jesus give His disciples in reference to the Spirit?

How can we receive the Spirit? What is the Holy Spirit parallel to in verse 13? What might this imply?

Study Matthew 10:5, 17-20, Mark 13:11, and Luke 12:11-12. During trials and persecution what will be the Spirit's ministry? How will He help disciples in their work?

7. The Spirit was prevalent in Jesus' ministry of exorcism. Notice the agent of the exorcisms in the following passages.

   Matthew 12:22-30

   Luke 10:17-21

8. Jesus declared that blasphemy against the Holy Spirit was unpardonable. Read Matthew 12:22-37, Mark 3:23-30, Luke 11:14-23, 12:8-10, and answer the following questions.

   What were the teachers of the law guilty of according to Jesus? Why do you suppose this is unforgivable? Why would not blasphemy against the Son of Man fall under the same category?

9. Write out principles you have gleaned from this study that would help you in the following situations.

   Expressing adoration to the Lord

   Understanding the unexplainable

   The necessary salvation of a loved one

Facing an overwhelming temptation

Articulating your faith

Desiring a spiritual gift

Opposing Satan

For Further Study
1. Using a concordance, look up any other references to the Spirit in the synoptic gospels and report your findings to your small group. What do these findings add to your knowledge of the Spirit?
2. Review the passages in the gospels, comparing two or three commentators' viewpoints. How do they compare with your own answers? Which commentator supports his reasoning the best and why?

•TOOL CHEST•
(A Suggested Optional Resource)

THE PERSON AND MINISTRY OF THE HOLY SPIRIT
Charles W. Carter's *The Person and Ministry of the Holy Spirit* (Schmul Publishing) is a systematic study of the Holy Spirit from a Wesleyan perspective. It researches the development of the doctrine of the Holy Spirit through the Scriptures categorically. Carter also explores the doctrines of Baptism with the Spirit in the Pentecostal tradition and the gifts of the Spirit. Other works you should advise are listed below.

> *The Holy Spirit* by Charles Caldwell Ryrie (Moody Press)
> *The Holy Spirit: His Person and Ministry* by Edwin Palmer
>   (Presbyterian and Reformed Publishing)
> *I Believe In the Holy Spirit* by Michael Green (Eerdmans)
> *What the Bible Says About the Holy Spirit* by Stanley M.
>   Horton (Gospel Publishing House)

3
Oil

• FOOD FOR THOUGHT •

Oil is a picture of the Holy Spirit that gives us rich expressions of His nature. Oil was extremely important to the people of Palestine. All sorts of industry depended on the olive oil produced in abundance in many areas of the country. The main service provided by the fruit of the olive tree was to provide light. The little clay lamps were filled with oil and lit at dark, making activity possible in the small homes or tents of the people.

Sometimes big torches fed by oil would be used to light the way through the narrow streets of the villages as a wedding procession made its way to the couple's new home. Such a wedding is graphically described for us in the Parable of the Ten Virgins in Matthew 25. Young women, friends of the bride, danced around her as they waited for the bridegroom to appear. There was always an element of surprise involved in a typical Palestinian wedding. No one knew just when the young man would make his appearance. It could be anywhere from one day to two weeks! The idea was to be ready for him at all times and not to be caught napping. Of course, no one stayed awake for two whole weeks, but the idea was to be prepared, making sure there was plenty of oil in the lamps!

In this particular parable, the best friend of the groom sounded out the warning at midnight that the bridegroom was coming. The wedding party woke up hurriedly and began to join the fun. The problem was half of them had allowed the oil in their lamps to run out.

There was no honeymoon as we know it in those days. Instead, the newlyweds held an open house for some of their choice friends. Those who received a personal invitation were invited to enjoy the festivities with the bride and groom. Once the bridegroom arrived at the house, the door was shut securely, and all who tried to gain admittance after that were steadfastly refused.

The immediate significance of this story involved the Jews. They certainly had been caught napping when Christ arrived in their midst! But the story has a universal warning as well. First, we learn that it is extremely dangerous to wait until the last minute to do business with God, and second, the parable is telling us that a person cannot "borrow" a relationship with Him. The five virgins who found their lamps empty asked their friends to give them some of their oil. They didn't get it. We cannot lend the Holy Spirit to another human being. It is our personal responsibility to make sure there is the oil of the Spirit in our lives. Otherwise it may well be that at Christ's second coming we will find the door shut against us and hear the voice of the bridegroom saying "I don't know you." So Jesus left us in no doubt as to the importance of having oil in our lamps or personally possessing the Holy Spirit.

The Bible also gives us plenty of hints as to the nature of oil. God gave Moses a recipe for the holy anointing oil used in the ritual of the tabernacle. We are told that it was to be made up of four specific spices. The perfumer was told to use myrrh, a costly and rare spice that was used in healing remedies, beauty treatments, and embalmment. Next sweet cinnamon was included that excelled as a fragrance. Cassia, the third spice, was taken from the bark of a tree. This spice speaks of purity or transparency. Finally, calamus was extracted from the reeds by the river. This fragrance was obtained by crushing or bruising.

Now these are powerful pictures. Before the priests could be anointed, the oil had to be obtained. And before the oil could be obtained, the spices had to be collected and extracted by bruising! Pentecost comes only after Passover. In the same way, Jesus had to be crushed by our sin before the fragrances of His precious life could be mixed with the oil of the Spirit and made available to us so we with the priests could be anointed for service!

The four specific spices I have named were to be blended with a hint of olive oil creating a unique blend. The priests knew how to make this totally distinctive perfume or oil, and the temptation must have been great to turn their hands to a quick buck. Why not make a little bit extra and sell it on the side? But God knows the heart of man and forestalled any intentions by forbidding such merchantry. It was not to be sold for profit by the perfumer in the back streets (Exodus 30:32-33). One reason for this was because the unique fragrance of the anointed person would single him out. There would be no doubt he had been near the heart of God.

The priests were also forbidden to make no cheap imitations. Man's ingenuity would enable him to imitate the smells and substance of the stuff, but God didn't want His picture spoiled! He wanted us to understand that the work of the Holy Spirit cannot be duplicated. Religious self effort will never pass, even at close scrutiny, for the Spirit's activity.

Lastly, the perfume was to be used for the family. It was for Aaron and his sons, and surely this speaks to us of the priesthood of all believers. In the Old Testament it was the Levites and their families that were set apart for God. Since Pentecost, all believers everywhere are priests, anointed by the Holy Spirit to do His work here on earth (Revelation 1).

So just how was this holy oil used in Old Testament times? Who was anointed and why? We have already mentioned that oil was used by the Levites and particularly the high priest and his sons. To qualify for this high calling of service these people had to be anointed. It was a sign and promise of the Lord's equipping. Of course he never calls without equipping. The scripture says "Faithful is He that calleth you who also will do it."

This oil was also used for healing purposes. When a leper was healed of his disease or a person had a skin problem and it cleared up, he was told to let the priest examine him. Then the healed person had to go to the tent of meeting with his sacrifice (Leviticus 14:22). This picture shows us that atonement comes before anointing for service. After he had examined the healed person, the priest would touch the man's ear saying, "Lord, I will hear for thee." Then he would touch the man's hand saying, "Lord, I will act for thee." Next he would touch the man's foot saying, "Lord, I will walk up and down, to and fro for thee." Finally, the priest would take the oil and pour it over the man's head so that it would flow freely all over his body—and say, "Thou art His that saves thee!" What an amazing thing—a leper with a ministry. All his life the leper would wonder about that incredible privilege. Cleansed, yet anointed to serve! Whenever I think about speaking, working, or acting for Him, I realize I am only a "cleansed leper" and am grateful beyond measure for His transforming, forgiving power in my life!

The holy oil was also used in the sanctuary where lamps on lamp stands gave light for worship. The lamps were placed in strategic positions and were to be kept lit at all times. In the same way, the light of the Holy Spirit illuminates our worship continually, helping us to "see" the God we worship. We cannot worship the Lord without our spiritual understanding being enlightened. When we come to the Word of God for help and pray David's prayer "Open my eyes that I see wonderful things in Your law" (Psalm 119:18). God asks the Holy Spirit to personally answer that prayer. I often tell audiences that we need to peek around the corner of a verse if the Scriptures are to live. It is around the corner of a verse we will often see someone standing in the shadows, smell the smells, or see the colors. However, imagination has its limits. I am well aware that though God has given me a vivid and creative imagination, I am totally dependent on the Holy Spirit to point out the point! He will help me apply the discoveries that He and I make together and show me how to help others to see His life-changing truth.

•TALKING IT OVER•

1. DISCUSS.

   10 minutes

   Discuss the importance of the oil to the 10 Virgins in Matthew 25.
   ☐ How do we obtain the oil?
   ☐ How do we know if we have the oil?
   ☐ Share an experience of the discovery of this truth.

2. REVIEW.

   10 minutes

   Review the different spices used to make the oil.
   ☐ Which spice picture spoke to you and why?
      Myrrh   Calamus   Cinnamon   Cassia

3. DISCUSS.

   10 minutes

   God gives us His "oil" for a purpose. Discuss each of these purposes.
   ☐ Equipping
   ☐ Healing
   ☐ Cleansing
   ☐ Worship

•PRAYING IT THROUGH•

1. (On your own) Read the account of the 10 Virgins in Matthew 25. Pray, asking God to show you if you possess the Holy Spirit. If you don't—invite Him to come into your life. If you do—thank Him that He came in.

   5 minutes

2. (As a group) Pray for people who don't possess the Spirit. Pray we will have the courage to tell them how to receive Him. Pray for evangelism around the world:
   □ Sports evangelism
   □ Film evangelism
   □ Music evangelism
   □ Church evangelism

   10 minutes

3. (In twos) Pray specifically for people you know who have need in the areas of:
   □ Ministry
   □ Healing
   □ Cleansing
   □ Worship

   5 minutes

• DIGGING DEEPER •

The Spirit and the Apostle John's Writings
This lesson will include the Apostle John's descriptions of the Spirit both in his Gospel and in his epistles.

1. Skim the book of John and observe the several names or designations given to the Spirit. In each case note the speaker who is referring to the Spirit and also the Spirit's activity. You may wish to consult a concordance. If time permits, read 1 John 3:24; 4:6, 13; 5:6-8.

Reference	Name	Speaker	Activity

2. Read John 3:1-21. What is the main thought or teaching of this passage? The key or repeating words should serve as a clue.

   What is being contrasted in this passage?

   After studying the context, consult a study Bible or commentary and list the possible interpretations for "born of water" (v. 5).

What does water *not* signify in this passage?

What is the Spirit's activity in regeneration according to this passage and 6:63?

What do verses 7-8 teach about the Spirit?

Give current examples of attempts to restrict the Spirit's work of rebirth.

From the context of this passage, what are the prerequisites to the Spirit's work of rebirth in a person's life?

Have you fulfilled these prerequisites? Do you know for certain that you have been reborn by the work of the Spirit? If you are not sure, write a simple prayer from your heart below asking the Spirit to work His second birth in your life.

3. Read John 14:15-31; 15:26; 16:5-16. What is the theme of each of these passages?

Review Jesus' explanation and description of the Spirit. Make a list of the Spirit's characteristics and functions.

Why can't the world recognize the Spirit?

What is the Spirit's ministry to believers?

What is His ministry to the world?

Reread John 14:15-27 and personalize this passage by reading as if it were written to you personally.

Looking over your list, which of these qualities means the most to you and why? How should this quality of the Spirit make a difference in your life today?

4. Review John 14:17; 1 John 3:24; 4:13. What precious truth do these verses teach? Do you sometimes doubt this truth? Consider meditating on these verses for a week. Write them out on 3 x 5 cards and place them where you will be frequently reminded of them.

5. Read John 20:21-22. When did the disciples receive the Spirit according to John?

From the context of these verses decide for what purpose the giving of the Spirit was linked.

What mission has God given to you? Do you rely on the Spirit to accomplish it?

For Further Study
1. Do a word study of *paraclete* (counselor). How is the word defined and interpreted? What does this tell you about the Spirit?
2. Memorize a verse from your lesson that was particularly enlightening. Repeat it to a friend.

•TOOL CHEST•
(A Suggested Optional Resource)

THE DISCIPLE'S STUDY BIBLE

The Disciple's Study Bible (Holman Bible Publishers) features the New International Version. It is unique from previous works of its kind in that its major emphasis is on tracing the development of 27 doctrines throughout the Bible. In the study notes at the bottom of each page the verse is indicated as well as a bold print indication to which doctrine this verse applies. For example, under John 14:15-21, the study note reads "Holy Spirit, Personal," giving an explanation.

Another important aspect of the *The Disciple's Study Bible* is the Life Helps section. This section seeks to help Bible students apply doctrines to everyday life, emphasizing how each relates to discipleship. It addresses many topics including how to worship, how to have a quiet time, meditation, and Christian counseling.

This Bible contains many other helps such as sermon outlines. It is set up superbly for topical Bible study. You may wish to look through one at your local Christian bookstore before making this major purchase.

4

Water

Water, streams, springs, wells, rivers, waterfalls—perfect pictures of the Holy Spirit! This symbol is found all through the Scriptures. Perhaps one of the best known places, however, is in John 4. This is the narrative that tells us of Jesus' encounter with a woman at Sycar's well.

The Lord, tired from His journey, rested at the well while His disciples went to buy food. Meanwhile, a Samaritan woman came to draw water. Jesus asked her to draw some for Him. The woman was amazed as she recognized His Jewish clothes and knew that Jews never had any dealings with the lowly Samaritans. The Lord never one to lose an opportunity to talk to someone about His Father said to her "If you knew the gift of God and who it is that asks you for a drink, you would have asked him and he would have given you living water" (John 4:10).

The Lord knew the woman was a thirsty, unsatisfied person. She had lived with five husbands, trying to quench an inner thirst she perhaps erroneously believed had to do with her relationship with men. The Lord also knew something else about her. He knew she didn't have to be thirsty. There is certain information God wants to pass on to all of us. He wants us to know Him, accept His gift of the Holy Spirit and never thirst again. The lady having received the information needed to respond. Jesus wanted her to ask Him for the living water that would quench her life thirst. He wanted her to ask Him personally. It wasn't only a matter of information but of appropriation.

The woman in the story didn't know that Jesus Christ and the Holy Spirit are like thirst-quenching water, but *we* know about these things. Perhaps we have heard the Spirit speaking to our hearts in a meeting or while reading a book. Or we have heard the invitation from a friend to drink from the spiritual fountain God has made available to us. The question we must face is not, "Do we know?" but, "Have we asked?" We need to personally apply this information before our thirst goes away. And this is a free gift! Isaiah knew this and used the symbol of water to urge his hearers to come to the waters and drink freely (Isaiah 55). If we literally don't know what to say, we can always borrow the very words of Scripture and say with the woman at the well, "Sir, give me this water so that I won't get thirsty and have to keep coming here to draw water" (John 4:15).

Jesus promises we will be satisfied if we do this. We will never thirst again. "Whoever drinks the water I give him will never thirst" (John 4:14). When Jesus said the Holy Spirit would be in us, He used the graphic picture of a spring-fed well for the people of His day. He knew the people understood what an absolute necessity water was. Water was life-giving, life-producing, life sustaining. It is harder for us living today in the modern western world to understand Jesus' graphic picture. Jesus was telling us we are not going to satisfy our spiritual thirst by mistaking it for other needs. If we lower our buckets down a well of men, houses, friends, dogs, hobbies, or even accomplishments, we will find ourselves thirsty at the end of the day. As the Psalmist puts it, "As pants the hart for cooling streams so pants my soul after thee, oh my God" (Psalm 42:1).

What a real experience of deep soul happiness we find when we receive from Christ the free gift of the Holy Spirit and find in Him an inexhaustible reservoir of life. Our job is then to come with our bucket of faith and let it into the well with the rope of prayer drawing up to ourselves spiritual blessings. Then, like the woman Jesus met at the well, we can leave our bucket at Jesus' feet and run back to our thirsty, needy world to share the *good news* with our friends. Have you been discovering the Holy Spirit is like a well of water? Then have you been sharing that water with the world? With joy, the Psalmist said, "Will we draw water from the wells of salvation?" The joy is very important. Not too many folks will be eager to accept a drink of anything from a person with a sour face!

But perhaps drawing water for other people out of your well really isn't your thing. Have you ever wondered why? Perhaps your well has been capped like the wells during Isaac's time. Some Philistines came along and dumped a whole lot of dirt down your well so the water couldn't flow out! If that's the case you'll need, like Isaac, to reopen the well dug previously so that thirsty people can find refreshment once more (Genesis 26:18). Then you will not only know the joy of the well in you, but you will experience the incredible satisfaction of rivers of life flowing out of you!

Jesus used this symbol of water in his teaching in the most graphic fashion one day in Jerusalem. The temple court in Jerusalem was packed with people on a certain Jewish feast day. At a particular point in the ceremony, the high priest paraded into a prominent place with a huge jar of water held high. He then poured it out in front of everybody, reminding them of when Moses smote the rock in the wilderness and water gushed out. It was at this dramatic juncture that Jesus rose to His feet and shouted, "If anyone is thirsty, let him come to me and drink. Whoever believes in me, as the Scripture has said, streams of living water will flow from within him" (John 7:37-38). That really got everybody's attention! The Bible points out for our benefit that "by this he meant the Spirit, whom those who believed in him were later to receive. Up to that time the Spirit had not been given, since Jesus had not yet been glorified" (John 7:39). Jesus spoke of a beautiful experience that can be ours. The smitten rock (Jesus) gives forth living water (the Spirit). All who are thirsty should listen, believe it, and drink. That's the first part. The second part is to allow the river full course through our lives.

The river of life is another much used picture in the Scriptures. The source of this river is the throne room in Heaven itself. Revelation 22 and Ezekiel 47 give us symbolic descriptions of this mighty life-giving river flowing from the heart of the throne of God. There is absolutely no other source of life. The picture also helps us to realize that the rivers of living water will only run out of our lives if God is on His throne in our hearts. Isaiah 32:1-2 tells us that when a king reigns then his subjects will be like watersheds diverting a blessing where ever it is needed.

The force of these life-giving blessings is immense. Ezekiel in chapter 47 talks of seeing himself paddling around in these waters, then wading in them, swimming in them, and finally in over his head! The idea here is to abandon yourself to the Spirit. Then the desert around us—in our home, our office, our town, our city, our country, will blossom like a rose. We can actually be the means of creating springs in our valleys!

My very favorite verse of Scripture is: "You will be like a well-watered garden, like a spring whose waters never fail," (Isaiah 58:11). So often people ask me, "How do you stay fresh, Jill? Who feeds you? Where do you get a drink?" The answer is very simple— from Him. There is within me a well, and if I do my job and keep it cleaned out then out of my innermost being will flow rivers of living water. He will indeed make my life like a beautiful well-watered garden. I wrote a prayer with these thoughts in mind. Let me share it with you.

WALK WITH ME

Here my friend
    walk with me
        around the garden
        of my life.

Smell the flowers,
    see the colors of my character
        blossoming in profusion
    where confusion used to be.
See the trees, tall and straight
    pointing up to heaven
        where before was thorn and briar, now a place for
birds to perch
    resting weary wing.
Stay awhile, meet my heavenly Gardener;
    see, it's Jesus sitting in the shade!
See the Spirit's shaft of light
    warming tired turf that knows
        renewal spreading down.

Take a look around—see how far I've come.
    I'm working on the weeds!
Gather a handful of daffodils before you go,
    yellow as heaven, fresh as my Jesus.
Take them home with you,
    think on them
        and pray for me
    as I for you, my friend—
        "Make us like a watered garden!"

•TALKING IT OVER•

1. DISCUSS GOD'S WELL OF WATER.   *15 minutes*
   ☐ How did you hear God's invitation to come and
   quench your spiritual thirst? Circle and share
   your answers.

   from the Spirit   the bride   the other believer
                      (church)

   ☐ What sort of prayer did you use to invite the
   Spirit within? Give examples.
   ☐ How do we get the water out of the well? With
   a rusty bucket, a frayed rope, or no energy?
   ☐ Name a few Philistines who have dumped dirt
   in your well! (e.g., the Philistine of laziness)

2. EXAMINE GOD'S RIVER OF LIFE.   *15 minutes*
   ☐ Read Revelation 22:1-2. Discuss these verses
   and share a picture you like from them.

   ☐ Read Ezekiel 47:1-12. Compare Ezekiel's vision with John's in Revelation 22:1-2. What aspects of the vision were the same? What aspects were different? What new thing do we
   learn about the river of life?

•PRAYING IT THROUGH•

1. (On your own) Praise Him for inviting you to
   quench your thirst and the way you found Jesus
   Christ. Pray about the "dirt" in your well that has
   taken your joy away. Repent. Ask Him to fill you
   again.

   3 minutes

2. (As a group) Pray for those who instruct believers
   how to draw water from the well (teachers, seminary professors, Sunday School leaders, youth
   leaders, writers).

   5 minutes

3. (In twos) Share a desert or valley situation. Pray
   with your partner for the people involved. Pray
   that the rivers will flow.

   5 minutes

4. (As a group) Pray for freshness in:
   ☐ your own life
   ☐ family life
   ☐ church life

   7 minutes

•DIGGING DEEPER•

The Spirit and the Book of Acts

The Book of Acts is not a theological presentation. Rather, it is the story of the development of the early burgeoning church and the Spirit's movement in the life of the church and disciples. Therefore, be cautious of basing a doctrine on any specific incident.

1. The Book of Acts places a tremendous emphasis on mission, the mission the Spirit directed the first disciples and Church to fulfill. Read the following references in Acts and take note of the context surrounding each. According to them, what was the prerequisite for mission?

   Acts 1:4-8

   Acts 2:4, 14

   Acts 8:34-40

   Acts 9:31

   Acts 10:19-48

   Acts 11:22-24

   Acts 13:1-4

2. To which group of people did the Spirit direct the spread of the Gospel in each of the above passages? (cf. 1:8)

Place	Group of People	Reference
Jerusalem:		
Judea:		
Samaria:		
Uttermost parts of the earth:		

3. According to the previous and subsequent references, what are some of the conditions for receiving the Holy Spirit?

   Acts 5:32

   Acts 10:44-46

4. What did the Spirit enable these men to do?

   Acts 2:1-4, 14

   Acts 4:8-12

   Acts 6:8-10

   Acts 8:26-40

   Acts 10:19ff

Acts 11:22-24

Acts 13:1-4

Acts 16:6-10

Acts 20:22-24

How does this relate to your previous study of John 20:21-22?

Which of these accounts fulfills the promise in John 15:26-27?

5. What else did the Spirit empower people for in Acts?

Acts 6:1-6

Acts 7:54-60

Acts 11:28; 21:11

Acts 13:9

Acts 13:51-52

Acts 15:28

Acts 20:28

6. The Spirit continued the following activity during the first century when Acts was written. Scholars are divided on whether this activity continues today and if so, in what form.

Acts 2:18

Acts 11:28

Acts 19:6

Acts 21:11

Study arguments on both sides of the issue and study the supporting evidence given (cf., commentaries on Acts, books on the Holy Spirit or theological dictionaries in your church or library). Is this an issue you can be dogmatic about? Why or why not?

7. Acts 5:1-11 reveals what concerning the Spirit's identity?

   5:3

   5:4

   5:9

8. Summarize in a paragraph what the Holy Spirit's role ought to be in:

   Evangelism

Selecting church leaders

Carrying out ministry

9. To whom is the Spirit directing you to share the Gospel?

10. Is there a particular ministry the Spirit has empowered you for? Are you actively serving in that ministry?

11. Recount the Spirit's activity in your own life.

For Further Study
1. Make a chart of the 28 chapters in Acts listing the Spirit's movement in each chapter.

•TOOL CHEST•
(A Suggested Optional Resource)

THE BOOK OF THE ACTS
The Book of the Acts (Eerdmans) by F.F. Bruce is a conservative commentary on Acts. It was written with Bible students and pastors in mind, but in a manner where lay people can take advantage of its wealth. For example, Greek references are found only in the foot-notes which allows for a more readable text for the English reader. You may wish to supplement your devotions and Bible study with the use of a commentary after you have done your own inductive study. The General Index and Index of Scripture References in the back of the volume will help you quickly locate material written on a specific topic or passage. Check this book out of a nearby Christian library before investing in such a major purchase.

5

Dove

John the Baptist witnessed a manifestation of the Holy Spirit in the form of a dove. Jesus had just come out of the water after being baptized when John saw this special symbol of the Holy Spirit (John 1:32). God had told John he would know the Messiah by this sign (John 1:33).

The occasion of Jesus' baptism marked the beginning of the Lord's earthly ministry. The anointing—a term used to designate God's selection, commissioning, and consecration given for a particular task—took place in the Jordan River. Most commentators link this event to the prophecy in Isaiah 61:1-3 where the prophet speaks of God's servant who was to come. When Jesus went to the synagogue in His home town after His baptism, He stood up and read that very passage from Isaiah saying, "Today this Scripture is fulfilled in your hearing" (Luke 4:18-19, 21). God had called Christ to redeem the world. He gave Him the power to do it by anointing Him with the Holy Spirit.

The Bible talks about an anointing like this for the believer. The Holy Spirit commissions us for a particular service. So often Christians say to me, "I know I'm a Christian, but I don't know what God wants me to do about it." The Dove has come to our hearts to tell us!

In 2 Corinthians 1:21 and 1 John 2:20-27, Paul and John respectively told the ordinary believers of their day that the anointing of the Spirit meant they would be taught to discern error and recognize false teachers. It also meant the Spirit would reveal spiritual truth to them apart from teachers and instructors. We are all encouraged to personally discern God's will for our lives. Along with this imparted knowledge will be a discovery of the gifts and abilities we have been given to get the job done.

62

The anointing of the Spirit also brings a grand assurance inside us. A certainty that all this is true, and that we can rely on the information the Holy Spirit will give us. We are also told that when the Dove has come, we have been "sealed" (Ephesians 1:13). In fact, the Spirit Himself is the seal. What does this mean? A seal on a signet ring was used like a stamp to transpose a man's signature. It spoke of authority and authenticity. The Spirit brands the believer in Jesus with just such a brand of belief, a reality of faith that tells a watching world, "This life is for real; it's no fake!"

The seal also speaks of ownership. A business transaction in Old Testament times would be sealed in front of witnesses and another party would be given the deeds to keep until they were claimed in the future. You can read a perfect example of this in Jeremiah 32:9-12. Jeremiah was under house arrest while the Babylonians were battering down the doors of his city. He was told by God to buy a piece of land and put the deeds of it in a clay jar in front of witnesses—the leaders of the land. God used this common day occurrence as a picture to Israel. He wanted them to clearly understand they were His purchased possession. In the future, that which was rightfully His (people created and redeemed by Himself) would belong to Him in a whole new way. They would enjoy future blessings and prosperity, even though at the moment all seemed lost as they faced many hard years in exile.

The Lord says we can find ourselves in this picture. "In him we were also chosen, having been predestined according to the plan of him who works out everything in conformity with the purpose of his will, in order that we, who were the first to hope in Christ, might be for the praise of his glory. And you also were included in Christ when you heard the word of truth, the gospel of your salvation. Having believed, you were marked in him with a seal, the promised Holy Spirit, who is a deposit guaranteeing our inheritance until the redemption of those who are God's possession—to the praise of His glory" (Ephesians 1:11-14).

When the Holy Spirit comes into our lives He is like a deposit given to us as a guarantee that the rest will be forthcoming. That's what the word *seal* means—a deposit guaranteeing what is to come.

The modern Greek word *seal* can be translated as an engagement ring. This seal or signet ring can be given as a pledge or promise of better things to come. And what are these better things to come for the Christian? They are the reality of Heaven instead of the mere hope of it. God gives us His engagement ring to help us realize the future wedding in Heaven is surely going to take place. The seal of

God speaks then of authenticity, ownership, and lastly security. This is not the place to discuss eternal security, but suffice it to say, God's word can be trusted. He promises and keeps that which He has promised.

I remember my husband giving me my engagement ring. I had wondered what he would say. I imagined some romantic Romeo-Juliet verbiage. Instead he placed the ring firmly on my finger and said emphatically, "Well, Jill, that's that!" It wasn't quite what I had been expecting, but I felt a lot better about it before the day was through. My mom had promised a friend we would buy the ring from her. As I entered our house with my new ring glistening on my finger, my mother was on the phone with her friend. Embarrassed, Mom thrust the receiver into my hands saying, "You explain!"

"I'm so sorry, Mrs. Conel," I spluttered. "We've already purchased the ring, but—but—maybe next time!"

It was then that my fiancé gently took the phone out of my hands, took me in his arms, and said firmly, "Jill, I told you—there won't be a next time. Remember, 'That's that'?"

Suddenly those two little words sounded like the most romantic words in the whole world! They gave us a sense of security that enabled us to build a healthy marriage together. If I can trust my husband's promises how much more can I trust God's. He said, "No one can snatch them out of my hand" (John 10:28).

So the gentle dove speaks of anointing and assurance, and lastly abuse! The dove is indeed a suitable symbol to remind us of the terrible possibility of grieving the Spirit of God who lives within us!

Think of the dove's nature. What a loving, peaceful, innocent, vulnerable creature he is. How open to abuse he has been throughout history. When John witnessed the Spirit descending on Christ setting Him apart for His work, he tells us he saw the Spirit resting and remaining on Him. "God," he said, "gave Christ the Spirit without limit" (John 3:34). God gives us the Spirit without limit too! The problem is that we can actually limit Him. When we do this we quench the Spirit, something we are specifically told not to do in 1 Thessalonians 5:19. The word *quench* means to suppress or subdue. The loving, gentle, nature of the Holy Spirit makes Him vulnerable to this type of abuse.

We can limit and quench Him when we exclude Him from decisions we make, when we keep Him out of our relationships, or when we limit His access to our thoughts. We limit the Spirit when we refuse to give Him first place in our affections.

The Bible tells us we can not only quench the Spirit, but we can grieve the Spirit too. Ruth Paxson in her book *Life on the Highest Plane* gives us a detailed list of ways we can grieve the Spirit of God:

HE is the Spirit of faith (2 Corinthians 4:13) so doubt, unbelief, distrust, worry, anxiety, grieve Him.

HE is the Spirit of grace (Hebrews 10:29) so that which is hard, bitter, ungracious, unthankful, malicious, unforgiving or unloving, grieves Him.

HE is the Spirit of holiness (Romans 1:4) so anything unclean, defiling or degrading, grieves Him.

HE is the Spirit of wisdom and revelation (Ephesians 1:17) so ignorance, conceit, arrogance and folly, grieve Him.

HE is the Spirit of power, love, and discipline (2 Timothy 1:7) so that which is barren, fruitless, disorderly, confused and uncontrolled, grieves Him.

HE is the Spirit of life (Romans 8:2) so anything that savors of indifference, lukewarmness, spiritual dullness, and deadness, grieves Him.

HE is the Spirit of glory (1 Peter 4:14) so anything worldly, earthly, or fleshly, grieves Him.

HE is the Spirit of truth (John 14:17) so anything false, deceitful, hypocritical, grieves Him.

The best example of lying to the Holy Spirit is that of Ananias and Sapphira who sold some land and brought half the proceeds to the Apostles for the needs of the church. Their sin was not in withholding half the proceeds for themselves but in the lie they told about it. They said they had given the whole proceeds to the Apostles, but as Peter pointed out, they had agreed together to lie to God, not to men (Acts 5:4). But Ananias and Sapphira died almost instantly when Peter exposed them, and great fear fell upon the whole church. I bet it did! When we say we have given the Lord our time, our money, and our love when we haven't, we can know we are grieving and abusing the Holy Spirit of God. He takes those sorts of lies very, very seriously indeed.

So we can quench, grieve, and limit the Spirit. We can also blaspheme the Holy Spirit. Let me say right away that if you are at all concerned that you have blasphemed the Holy Spirit—you haven't! Such a concern would not be felt by one who has. This sin is only mentioned in Mark 3, Luke 12, and Matthew 12. The context makes it clear it is not a serious moral lapse or insulting God or Jesus due to rebellion or ignorance. There are basically two schools of thought about this unforgivable sin. One view is that it is a willful conscious rejection of God's activity and an attributing such to Satan. In other words—a person who chooses to call the works of God the works of the devil. The other school is that one blasphemes the Holy Spirit when he repudiates the Spirit's call to Christ as the one and only way of salvation. This sin cannot be forgiven and Augustine held that "all who are finally impenitent are guilty of it."

Oswald Sanders says that blaspheming the Holy Spirit is not a sin of ignorance. God has not set a mysterious line over which one may unwittingly cross (*The Holy Spirit of Promise*, p. 133). He says that this sin is unforgivable because it rejects forgiveness and, therefore, there is no provision for it! Enough to say if you have not responded to the gentle voice of God's dove, don't gamble on the goodness of God. Better to come to Him at once in case you cross the fatal line.

•TALKING IT OVER•

Suggested Times

1. READ AND DISCUSS THE ANOINTING OF THE SPIRIT.
   Read the account of Jesus being anointed in John 1:29. Discuss its significance.

   7 minutes

2. REVIEW THE ASSURANCE OF THE SPIRIT.
   Which aspect of the Seal helps you most and why?
   ☐ Ownership
   ☐ Authentication
   ☐ Security
   ☐ Deposit

   7 minutes

3. STUDY THE ABUSE OF THE SPIRIT.
   Which aspect of the abuse of the Spirit concerns you most and why?
   ☐ Quenching
   ☐ Grieving
   ☐ Resisting
   ☐ Blaspheming

   8 minutes

4. MEDITATE ON ACTS 5.
   Meditate on the story of Ananias and Sapphira. Talk about it.

   8 minutes

• PRAYING IT THROUGH •

Suggested Times

1. (On your own) Give praise for the Dove since the Dove has come.

   5 minutes

2. (As a group) Pray that:
   - [ ] God will raise up more dynamic preachers and teachers.
   - [ ] Their faith will be real.
   - [ ] They may have a sense of inner security and stability.
   - [ ] That they may keep their eyes on Heaven!

   10 minutes

3. (On your own) Take a moment and meditate on any sin of abuse of the Spirit in your life. Then pray for:
   - [ ] Those you know who are willfully grieving the Spirit.
   - [ ] People who are living a lie.

   5 minutes

•DIGGING DEEPER•

The Spirit and the Letters of Paul

1. The Holy Spirit was very real and personal to Paul. He was the foundation from which Paul operated. From these passages how did Paul regard his own ministry?

Romans 15:19

1 Corinthians 2:4-5

1 Corinthians 2:6-10

1 Corinthians 2:13

1 Corinthians 7:40

2 Corinthians 3:3-11

2 Corinthians 6:6

Ephesians 3:2-6

1 Thessalonians 1:5

What is the basis of *your* ministry? (i.e., your motivation, energy, enthusiasm, joy, purpose)

2. Read 1 Corinthians 2:1-16. List several aspects of the Spirit's ministry.

Which of these characteristics are you lacking?

3. According to the following verses, what does the Spirit have to do with our salvation?

Romans 2:28-29

Romans 5:1-5

Romans 8:1-4

Romans 8:9

Romans 8:14-15, 23

1 Corinthians 6:11

2 Thessalonians 2:13

Titus 3:5-6

How does this correlate with what you have learned in previous Digging Deeper sections?

4. God the Father has adopted us by the agency of the Holy Spirit. What facts can you state about adopting a baby today?

What do these verses teach about adoption?

Romans 8:14-17, 23

Galatians 4:6-7

Ephesians 1:5

Jot a note to your heavenly Father telling him what your adoption means to you.

5. Look up these terms in a Bible dictionary and an English dictionary and briefly describe how each relates to the Spirit.

Seal (2 Corinthians 1:22; Ephesians 1:13-14)

Deposit (2 Corinthians 1:22; 5:5)

First fruits (Romans 8:23)

How is the Spirit a guarantee of what is to come? What would this have meant to first-century readers? Can you think of a contemporary example of first fruits? How does this metaphor (*first fruits*) for the Holy Spirit encourage you?

6. Turn to the term *sanctification* in a Bible dictionary and give a shortened definition.

How does Paul view the Spirit's role in our sanctification?

Romans 7:6

Romans 8:5-27

Romans 9:1

Romans 14:17-18

Romans 15:13-16

1 Corinthians 6:11

1 Thessalonians 1:4-6

2 Thessalonians 2:13

2 Timothy 1:14

1 Peter 1:2

7. The Christian life is demanding. How does the Spirit equip and enable us to live an obedient life?

Romans 8:4-6

Galatians 3:3

Galatians 5:5

Galatians 5:16-18

Galatians 5:22-26

Ephesians 3:16

What adjectives would you use to describe the Christian life? Give examples of living this life by human effort.

8. Review your answers to this lesson using them as a check list. For example, is your mind controlled by the Spirit? Do you rely on the Holy Spirit's help to pray, to convict your conscience,

and to teach you God's wisdom? Spend time this week asking God to help you live a Spirit-led life.

For Further Study
1. Complete a concordance study on the Holy Spirit in Paul's letters and see what more you can discover about his ministry.
2. Memorize a verse from this lesson that was particularly meaningful to you.

•TOOL CHEST•
(A Suggested Optional Resource)

THE PURSUIT OF HOLINESS

The Holy Spirit was given to believers for many reasons, one being to help sanctify us or to set us apart as distinct from the world. This work involves the process of becoming holy. But how does one pursue holiness? Is it something which the Spirit bestows on us and which we passively receive? *The Pursuit of Holiness* (NavPress) by Jerry Bridges suggests this is not the case. This practical tool will help you understand the hand in hand role of the Spirit and your responsibility in developing a holy life.

6
Gifts

"Give us the tools, and we'll finish the job," said Winston Churchill referring to the weapons England would need to win the war against Germany. "Give them the gifts and they'll finish the job!" says the Father to the Holy Spirit, referring to the tools the church will need to win the war against evil. Spiritual gifts are very important. For the church concerned with the evangelization of the world, it is an exercise in futility to try and serve God's cause without exercising spiritual gifts.

The Giver of the gifts is God himself. He has demonstrated His generosity by the way He gave the world the greatest gift of all—His only Son (John 3:16). He delights in giving good gifts to His children. He not only gave His only Son but also His Holy Spirit, and seeing "God was in Christ reconciling the world to himself," we see the Father give us Himself as well (2 Corinthians 5:19). God's great gifts of love and life are quality gifts.

Not only did God give us himself, but He gave us "tools" or spiritual abilities. First of all, God gave the church gifts in the shape of leaders. These particular people are called apostles, prophets, evangelists, and pastor-teachers. They build up the body of Christ into maturity and prepare the church for works of service (Ephesians 4:11-12).

Some believe an apostle was one who saw Christ in the flesh and witnessed His resurrection. However, others such as Paul, Junias, and Andronicus who are called apostles did not see Him. The name *apostle* means a messenger—"one sent forth with orders" (Thayer). Other scholars believe that apostles were not an order destined to die out, but rather accredited messengers such as Barnabas who were commissioned by a church community. They would be the equivalent of our theologians today. An apostle's main task was to preserve the purity of Christian doctrine and redefine it for the present time.

A prophet, according to 1 Corinthians 14:3, edified, exhorted, and comforted Christians. Today, we would call that Spirit-empowered preaching. Both men and women received and exercised this gift as indicated by Philip's four daughters in Acts 21:9. Evangelists, on the other hand, preached to unbelievers, gathered the converts together, and established churches. They would be similar to today's evangelists and pioneer missionaries.

The pastor-teacher was a shepherd, gifted to protect the flock from hostile forces, *and* feed the sheep—interpreting the Word of God for them. There was no New Testament in those days so the pastor-teacher was very, very important. These people were given to the local assembly in order to help believers discover and develop their own spiritual abilities.

The gifts of the laity are described and demonstrated for us in the Scriptures. If the leaders I have just described are doing their job, three things will happen. First, people will discover and allow for the diversity of gifts. People are different and the Holy Spirit takes this into account, dividing the very different gifts of the Spirit to them "as he determines" (1 Corinthians 12:11). Christians should not insist on others having the same gift as theirs. Neither should they be jealous of each other. Paul uses an illustration of the different members of a body having their own functions (1 Corinthians 12).

The second thing that should happen is that the local assembly should understand that gifts are for the common good, and in order to keep unity in the church, they should be exercised in love without a competitive spirit. Third, the Holy Spirit's sovereignty is affirmed. Seeing He is the one who gives out the gifts, no one has the right to insist on another seeking a gift as often happens in the case of the gift of speaking in tongues. Someone has said there are two heresies regarding tongues—one is "you must" and the other is "you mustn't!"

Let's look at a list of spiritual gifts from the main passages that speak about them, recognizing that these lists are by no means exhaustive. Having talked about the first four, we can highlight the rest as follows.

There is the gift of government or rulings. The word *used* means the "steersman of a ship" or "one who stands in front as a leader." Then there is the gift of exhortation which is the ability to help people to act on the truth taught (Romans 12). There is the gift of giving. This, like many other gifts, is a gift bestowed on all of us, but for some it is the grace given to give vast wealth away. The gift of mercy with cheerfulness is that gift of practical love for those in distress; a gift to do with social needs. The word of wisdom and knowledge parallels the gift of the modern counselor. This is a supernatural ability to gain direct insight into spiritual truth, and find practical applications of it, not necessarily from Scripture. Then there is the gift of faith. Not saving faith in this instance, but faith that turns vision into fact. This sort of faith is demonstrated in the lives of those who trust God literally to supply their every need. For example, George Mueller who saw God supply food for his orphaned children.

There are gifts of healing and gifts of miracles, which are displays of power that go beyond the natural, and there is a gift of discerning of spirits that is vital today as we need to know what is divine and what is demonic. How necessary to be able to see what is the spirit of truth and what is the spirit of error! Then there is the gift of helps that relieves the poor, the sick, the aged and the helpless, and may have reference to the work of deacons. This gift is more than mere helpfulness but a special Spirit-led ability to give assistance. There is also the controversial gift of tongues, along with a gift of singing and blessing in the spirit, a gift that needs to be kept well in control. Paul says this gift is to be exercised in an orderly manner, and publicly only in order to edify the body. There are also three lesser known gifts. One of celibacy (1 Corinthians 7:7), another of voluntary poverty (Acts 2:45; 4:34), and the gift of martyrdom (1 Corinthians 13:3). The early church considered them gifts in the sense of God giving them this opportunity and spoke of them as such.

So how do we discover our gifts? Volunteer to fill a need without worrying if you can. You'll soon find out if you're gifted! Next consecrate your known talents. Let your leaders and other Christians help you to learn what your special spiritual abilities are. Pray about it.

However, you'll certainly need to watch for the dangers. Never become more interested in the gift than the Giver. Don't envy others' gifts, and don't abuse the gifts God has given you or use them for your own ends. For example, it's possible to use your speaking gifts for self engrandizement. As someone has said, "The answer to abuse is not misuse but right use!" May we all learn just how the Holy Spirit has gifted us and begin using those treasures for the glory of God.

•TALKING IT OVER•

1. SHARE.   *5 minutes*
   Make a list of your talents. Tell the group what
   they are.

2. REVIEW AND DISCUSS.   *5 minutes*
   Do you know your spiritual gift? What is it? Re-
   view 1 Corinthians 12:28-31 and discuss the gifts
   mentioned. Which are the most important and
   why?

3. READ   *10 minutes*
   Read 1 Corinthians 14 together.
   ☐ Which part of this chapter is most meaningful
     to you and why?
   ☐ What are the warnings you find?

4. DISCUSS.   *10 minutes*
   Discuss ways the church can help us to discover
   our gifts and ways we can help the church once
   they are discovered!

•PRAYING IT THROUGH•

Suggested
Times

1. (As a group) Praise the Father for: *5 minutes*
   - ☐ Jesus Christ
   - ☐ The Holy Spirit
   - ☐ His gifts

2. (As a group) Pray for: *5 minutes*
   - ☐ Your church
   - ☐ Your church leaders
   - ☐ Your church laity

3. (In twos) Pray for the use of spiritual gifts: *5 minutes*
   - ☐ In your church
   - ☐ In your community
   - ☐ In the world

4. (On your own) Pray about the abuse of spiritual gifts.   *5 minutes*

•DIGGING DEEPER•

The Spirit and the Gifts

1. Fill in the chart below listing the gifts of the Spirit, their purpose, results, and the surrounding context of each passage.

Reference	Gifts	Purpose	Results	Context
Romans 12:6-8				
1 Corinthians 12:8-10				
1 Corinthians 12:28				
1 Corinthians 13:1-3				
1 Corinthians 14:1ff				
Ephesians 4:11f				
1 Peter 4:11				

Notice the similarities and dissimilarities among the lists.

Are the lists of gifts meant to be exclusive? Did Paul intend them to be? Why or why not?

Can you discern any order of priority in each list of gifts?

2. Review each passage along with your observations. What factors about the gifts are important to Paul and Peter?

What categories or distinctions do you observe between lists?

3. Compare the gifts listed in the New Testament passages with your study of the Spirit in the Old Testament (Chapter One). Which gifts apparently functioned before the Spirit permanently indwelt believers?

Compare the purposes of the gifts in both Testaments. What is the relation of the Spirit's activity in the Old and New Testaments?

4. Focusing specifically on 1 Corinthians 12, make a list of all the facts you can glean concerning the Spirit and the gifts.

   What repeating principle do you find? Why do some people receive certain gifts over others?

   Define the gift of faith according to the broader context of this chapter.

   How may the gifts be misused?

5. Many debate whether some of the spiritual gifts are still operative today. Do you see any scriptural evidence to support either side of this issue?

6. Little teaching is given in these several passages on how to know your spiritual gift. Reflect on the chief purposes of the gifts. Why were they given? What good do they serve? What needs do they meet?

   What are the needs of your Christian community? How might this knowledge assist you in discovering your gift(s)?

Whom do you know who might help you discover and use your gift(s) to serve the Lord more effectively?

7. How do we reconcile these two phrases: The Spirit "gives them [gifts] to each one, just as he determines" (1 Corinthians 12:11) and "Desire the greater gifts"? (1 Corinthians 12:31)

8. What makes a person "spiritual"? What false standards have you used to measure another person's spiritual status? Your own spiritual status? According to 1 Corinthians, what standard should we use to determine spirituality?

    Why are the gifts expendable? In contrast, what is not expendable?

9. What have you learned about spiritual gifts? What unanswered questions about the gifts do you have? Where could you go for help?

For Further Study
1. Identify the needs of your Christian fellowship. Select one to fill. Find the appropriate manner to do so (i.e., consult your pastor, etc.). Ask a friend to pray with you daily as you seek to serve God in this new way. After a time, consult with your pastor and prayer partner regarding your effectiveness. Determine what further training would assist your doing a better job. Seek God's confirmation through Scripture, a wise counselor or pastor, your prayer partner, and those affected by your service. Decide if you have found your spiritual gift.

•TOOL CHEST•
(A Suggested Optional Resource)

DISCOVERING YOUR SPIRITUAL GIFTS
InterVarsity Press publishes a series of booklets as helps for understanding and living the Christian life. They are superb resources and make super gifts for friends, shut-ins, or hospitalized people. J.E. O'Day's *Discovering Your Spiritual Gifts* (InterVarsity) booklet on spiritual gifts concisely defines the gifts and gives suggestions for discovering, developing, and using your gift. These booklets are available at your local Christian bookstore.

7

Fruit

• FOOD FOR THOUGHT •

One of the most familiar symbols of the Holy Spirit is that of fruit. "The fruit of the Spirit," says Paul, "is love, joy, peace, patience, kindness, goodness, faithfulness, gentleness and self-control. Against such things there is no law" (Galatians 5:22-23). It's a graphic picture and an easy one for us to understand.

Paul begins the passage that contains these famous words with the phrase, "So I say, live by the Spirit, and you will not gratify the desires of the sinful nature" (Galatians 5:16). The verb "live" is in the present tense, reminding us that Paul is talking about habitual conduct, a present tense Christianity that doesn't live its life out in memories of past church-going, but vibrates with vitality in the here and now. If we live under the Spirit's sway, we won't be "feeding a need" with wrong food. We'll be feeding our souls with the Word and seeing spiritual results.

Paul explains that the reason for this conflict of interests between the old and new natures inside a Christian is that the old "us" wants to go on being the old "us," while the new nature of Christ, imparted by the Holy Spirit, wants to be Himself! He urges us not to give in to the selfish, insistent voice that tells us to shut our ears to the Spirit's promptings and do our own thing, but rather to heed God's whisper and obey His Word.

I like the idea of the Spirit prompting us to right living. Seeing I enjoy drama very much, I am very familiar with the prompter. He or she stands in the wings, eyes fastened to the script. The script says what should be said and done on stage. If the actors stumble, the prompter is quick to prompt so that the people in the limelight can do and say the right things in front of the audience.

I remember being at a party shortly after I came to faith in Christ. As the evening wore on, it became apparent that things were getting out of hand. The "flesh" or the "old me" wanted very much to stay and join in the fun, but the Spirit standing in the wings of my life prompted me to do the right thing, say the right words, and not depart from God's script for the evening. It was up to me to obey the Spirit's promptings. I'm glad I did.

Because we are under grace we have the free choice to obey or not to obey. But being under grace and not under the law certainly does not mean we are free from all moral authority. Paul in fact warns, "Do not use your freedom to indulge the sinful nature" (Galatians 5:13). The Old Testament system simply meant the people had no enablement to resist the power of sin. Now—this side of the cross, grace enables us, and the Holy Spirit empowers His promptings! So we are to keep in step with the Spirit. We are not to run ahead, neither are we to lag behind. It's a matter of keeping up with all the Lord is asking of us.

But how do we do that? I'm glad you asked! Fed by the Word, and led by the Spirit, we will find the grace to go on. To go on with the Lord means to grow the fruit of His character in our lives; to grow "love, joy, peace, patience, kindness, goodness, faithfulness, gentleness and self-control" (Galatians 5:22-23). As Paul puts it, "Serve one another in love. . . . If you keep on biting and devouring each other, watch out or you will be destroyed by each other" (Galatians 5:13, 15).

So what is this fruit of the Spirit we are free to grow in our lives? Fruit is the symbol of acts of love. The fruits of the "old" nature are obvious and ought not to be displayed on a good tree. This sort of behavior is described for us in Galatians 5:19. This long list of trouble talks about sexual, spiritual, social, and selfish sins. Filthy and indecent actions, wild parties and the like are out for the believer while the fruit of the Spirit manifests itself in faithfulness to one's partner in marriage. Love and self-control are in. God would have us sexually moral, pure, controlled, and clean.

The spiritual sins of idolatry and witchcraft, "spiritualism that encourages the acts of demons" (Galatians 5:19, LB) are out! The Christian is to take notice of the Word of God rather than horoscopes. The fruit of the Spirit will produce Godlikeness in us.

Social sins, fits of rage, discord, dissensions and factions are the fruit of the old tree. I like the way the *Living Bible* puts it, "The feeling that everyone else is wrong except those in your own little group" is the fruit of the old life (Galatians 5:20). These sort of problems in the body of believers cause people to 'bite and devour' one another. Or as the *Living Bible* says, "always be critical and catty!" Kindness, on the other hand, gives everyone the benefit of the doubt, and pressures us to try to be peacemakers. For the fruit of the Spirit is kindness and peace, tolerance and gentleness.

Paul explains that Christians are people who have nailed their evil desires to His cross and crucified them there. Someone has said that Christ's cross was a great symbol in itself, to remind us the selfish "I" has been crossed out!

How then is the fruit of the Spirit produced? By refusing to feed wrong needs and obeying the promptings of the Holy Spirit. He will use His Word—described as a sword—to prick our conscience and help us to strive habitually to conduct our lives according to love.

In John 15, Jesus talked about fruit. He told us to persevere constantly in this regard. He exhorted us to resort frequently to Him. Our lives will produce nothing but leaves if we don't. The fruit of Godliness will bring great honor to the Vine and this is what it's all about! If we want to please God, then we need to produce fruit. And not just a little deed of kindness here, or a loving pat on the shoulder there, but more fruit all the time until He sees much fruit! The expectation of the husbandmen is for a great harvest in our lives.

He will prune us and dig us about and set our faces toward the sun. He will see to it we are well watered and carefully and lovingly cultivated. When He looks our way, may He find more than rustling leaves; a mere show of spirituality. May we yield to His pruning and know the hand that holds the knife is a wounded one—wounded for you and me.

•TALKING IT OVER•

1. DISCUSS.   *10 minutes*
   - ☐ "Don't feed a need or a greed; it will swallow you up." Is this statement true or false?
   - ☐ What is a "prompting of the Spirit"? Give an example.

2. READ TOGETHER.   *10 minutes*
   Read Galatians 5 together. Which aspect of the fruit of the Spirit is hardest for you to exhibit? Why?

3. READ AND DISCUSS.   *10 minutes*
   Read John 15. Discuss each of the following:
   - ☐ The commands
   - ☐ The warnings
   - ☐ The promises
   Which verse from today's lesson will you take with you?

•PRAYING IT THROUGH•

Suggested Times

1. (As a group) Read Galatians 5:22-23. Praise God   *10 minutes*
   for the Holy Spirit's work. Pray for:
   ☐ People showing the fruit of their sinful nature.
   ☐ Different aspects of the fruit of the Spirit for
      different people.
   ☐ Each other.

2. (On your own) Meditate on John 15. Pray on your   *10 minutes*
   own or in twos for "abiding" principles to be evi-
   dent in your life. Pray for your family.

•DIGGING DEEPER•

The Spirit and the Fruit

1. Do a word study on *fruit*. Consult an exhaustive concordance for Old and New Testament references to fruit. Make a list of the various ways the word is used. Notice how Jesus used it. Also note how different New Testament authors used the terms. What similarities and dissimilarities do you observe?

   Review the usages of the word *fruit*. Then determine one generic meaning that would apply to all occurrences of the word. How does the use of *fruit* in Galatians 5:22 relate to your generic definition?

2. Read Galatians 5–6. In one or two sentences, state the overall theme.

3. Briefly title the paragraphs of Galatians 5–6, capturing their main emphases. List your paragraph titles. Do you detect a pattern or an outline developing?

4. What is the chief idea of Galatians 5:22-26? How does this correspond to the overall theme of chapters 5–6? How does this relate to what immediately precedes and follows this paragraph?

5. Focusing specifically on the list of fruit mentioned, can you conclude any order of priority within the list? What other Scripture(s) might shed light on this question?

Can you determine any categories or groupings among the fruit?

With what is fruit contrasted? Does this signify anything about its meaning in this particular passage?

6. What imperative is given? Are any practical instructions given for how to live out this command, either in the immediate or broader context of chapters 5–6?

Is verse 26 just an afterthought? Explain.

7. Does a person instantaneously receive the fruit or is it developed through process? What does the metaphor of fruit itself

suggest? How do we get the fruit? Support your answer from Scripture.

8. Select one fruit by which you would like to be characterized. Do a word study on this fruit repeating the steps already used in this lesson.

How would your life be different if you were characterized by this fruit? What difference would there be in your relationships, ministry, or work?

9. What action will you take this week to keep in step with the Spirit?

10. Why do you think Galatians 6:9-10 are included in Paul's discussion of living in accordance with the Spirit?

For Further Study
1. Memorize Galatians 5:22-26.
2. Each week do a word study on a new fruit.

•TOOL CHEST•
(A Suggested Optional Resource)

SPIRIT LIFE

Stuart Briscoe's *Spirit Life* (Revell) is a layman's commentary on each fruit of the Spirit listed in Galatians 5:22. It is filled with practical helps for living a life which gives evidence to the Holy Spirit's leading. Study questions are provided at the end of each chapter lending the book to a small group Bible Study or a book discussion group. Or, your Sunday School class would greatly benefit from a quarter of study in *Spirit Life.*

8
Cloud

• FOOD FOR THOUGHT •

Ephesians 5:15-21 tells us that being filled with the Spirit needs to be an ongoing experience for the believer. The command, "be filled," is in the present tense. This indicates that the fullness of the Spirit is not a once and for all experience. As the occasion requires, the Spirit repeatedly empowers for worship and ministry. When we obey God's command to be filled, His glory fills our soul and He cannot be hidden! He is seen in residence!

Many people argue about the subject of the fullness of the Holy Spirit. I take the point of view that the *fruit* of the Spirit, not necessarily the *gifts* of the Spirit, is evidence of His fullness. But I do agree that there *should* be evidence!

In the Old Testament, the presence of God was manifested by a cloud that symbolized the fullness of His glory. The cloud—or Shekinah glory of God—was to serve as a "shelter and shade from the heat of the day, and a refuge and hiding place from the storm and rain" (Isaiah 4:6). In Colossians 1:27, we learn that Christ in us is our hope of glory. Both Ezekiel and John saw in a vision a manifestation of that canopy of glory over the very throne of God. Christ Himself while here on earth showed Peter, James, and John a little glimpse of the glory of the Lord when He was transfigured before them on the Mount of Transfiguration. "We beheld His glory," John exults in 1 John 1. We can reflect that same glory as we allow Him to transform us into His image. This happens when we obey His Word and are continually full of the Holy Spirit. First, let's think about the fullness of the Spirit and then about the glory of the Lord.

If God commands us to be filled, the experience cannot be a feeling. It would be most unfair of God to command us to have a feeling. Rather, the command concerns control. Paul uses the illustration of drinking having control or power over a person (Ephesians 5). The person makes a conscious choice and effort to drink; the drink does the rest. The liquor affects the behavior of the person in such a way that it is obvious to all he or she is "under the influence."

I am not saying for a moment you won't feel anything when the Spirit's fullness controls your life, but godly character and spiritually-effective service will be parts of your experience as well. This was demonstrated by Elizabeth and Zechariah, who were both filled with the Spirit (Luke 1:6). They showed compassion to Mary and witnessed to everyone in sight. John the Baptist, "filled with the Holy Spirit even from birth" (Luke 1:15), and Simeon, filled with the Spirit also (Luke 2:25), were moved to be His voice to Israel. When we are filled with the Holy Spirit, the consuming passion of our lives will be to know Him and make Him known! The fullness of the Spirit then is obviously a present necessity.

The fullness of the Spirit is also the result of obedience. Obeying God's command results in a mutual encouragement to praise God and develop healthy mutual relationships with other people (Ephesians 5:19-20). We will find ourselves working on all these things doing the will of God from our hearts (Ephesians 6:6). Instead of wanting others to serve us, we will be full of ideas about serving others, with a submission of spirit that will be quite unusual.

Now this "full" experience is for everyone—not just the "super saints." Ephesians 5–6 addresses husbands, wives, children, slaves, and masters. In case you feel you're not in one of those categories, Paul adds the category "one another"! Not only is this for every Christian, but a life lived in the fullness of the Spirit will be perfectly natural and sweetly fragrant. It will have a definite impact on those around. To some it will be very attractive and to others extremely offensive! People will not be able to be neutral or indifferent to you.

When we are full of the Spirit we will experience a greater sensitivity to sin and a risk-taking ability that may be quite contrary to our whole personality—a volunteerism that is definitely not us! I remember inviting all my friends to a Christmas party in order to tell them about my conversion, knowing full well that I was inviting them not only to the party but to leave me! They accepted both invitations, but I survived the rejection pretty well! This sort of risk-taking was certainly against my normal bent. We lose our fullness, however, when we sin. Be careful to note I did not say, "We lose the Spirit when we sin." We lose the fullness of the Spirit—the manifestation of His presence in and through our lives. Nowhere is this more graphically illustrated than in the Old Testament.

The Shekinah glory of the Lord was a supernatural cloud which made an appearance to man in a form they could see! What is God's glory? His fullness, the self-revelation of Jehovah. This glory was shown to Moses at his own request: "Now show me your glory" (Exodus 33:18). Moses actually saw the form of Jehovah with his physical eyes. A cloud accompanied that manifestation. God's glory then is a physical manifestation of His divine presence.

In his vision of God's throne, Isaiah observed that "the temple was filled with smoke" (Isaiah 6:4). John saw the same thing hundreds of years later (Revelation 15:8). The cloud made its appearance when the law was given at Sinai (Exodus 33). When Moses had finished everything that he had started for the work of the tabernacle, then the cloud came bringing God's glory. Sometimes the glory of the Lord was so intense even the priests couldn't enter the holy precincts because of it (2 Chronicles 5:14; 7:1-3).

But it is in Ezekiel 9:3 that we have the most graphic picture of God's glory. Ezekiel saw God's glory depart from the temple. Why? Apparently, idols of Asherah, the Canaanite goddess of fertility and animals, were actually being worshiped in Jehovah's house. Tamnuz, a Babylonian fertility god, was also being honored. Sun worshipers too abounded in God's house and those who "put the branch to the nose"(Ezekiel 9)—a ceremonial gesture used in nature worship. This represented pantheism in God's domain. All these practices were detestable to the Lord. No wonder the glory of the Lord departed! How sad that the hardened Israelites didn't even realize God's glory was departing. They continued as if all was well!

Has the glory of the fullness of the Lord departed from your body, God's temple? If so, why? Do you even know whether God's glory is present in your life? You can be sure others will know it before long. No fruit will be evidenced. Yes, gifts which are not affected by sin will still perhaps be exercised, but the sweet manifestation of His presence will be strangely lacking and without a doubt His name will be dishonored.

May we all be found faithfully facing the Son, that we may be transformed into His image from glory to glory. May the blessing of the fullness of the glory of the Lord be ours!

•TALKING IT OVER•

1. REVIEW.   *5 minutes*
Which symbol means the most to you and why?

Fire	Wind	Oil	Water	Dove
	Gifts	Fruit	Cloud	

---

2. DISCUSS.   *15 minutes*
How do we obey the command to be filled with
the Spirit? Read Ephesians 5:18-33.
☐ Which is your favorite verse?
☐ Which is your least favorite verse?

As you review the experiences of Elizabeth,
Zechariah, and Simeon, notice any similar re-
sponses to being filled with the Spirit (Luke 1–2).

---

3. READ AND DISCUSS.   *10 minutes*
Read and discuss Romans 8:18-21; Romans 9:23;
1 Corinthians 2:7; 2 Corinthians 4:17. How
should this future hope affect us now? Discuss the
statement, "We cannot lose the Spirit, but we can
lose the fullness." Which aspect of the "glory
cloud" will you take away with you?

•PRAYING IT THROUGH•

Suggested Times

1. (On your own) Ask the Lord to first cleanse your heart, then praise Him for "everything," giving thanks.

5 minutes

2. (As a group) Pray for:
   ☐ Singing hearts
   ☐ Serving hearts
   ☐ Submissive hearts

5 minutes

3. (On your own) Quietly meditate on 2 Corinthians 3:12-18. After several minutes, praise God for the things you have been meditating on.

5 minutes

4. (In twos) Pray that the glory of the Lord will not depart from:
   ☐ Your church
   ☐ Your life
   ☐ The world

5 minutes

•DIGGING DEEPER•

The Spirit and Fullness

1. Read Ephesians 5:18. The verb, *be filled*, in the Greek is in the present tense referring to a continuous state. What does this fact indicate about the Spirit's filling?

2. What type of statement is, "be filled with the Spirit"? To whom is it directed? What does this imply about our responsibility?

3. How is it possible for a Christian to disobey this imperative? Do you ever treat it as an option? How could you actively pursue meeting the requirements of this command?

4. With what is being filled with the Spirit contrasted? How are they different?

5. Study the context surrounding Ephesians 5:18. Describe the four-fold effect of the Spirit's fullness.

6. What does Spirit-filled speech center around?

Consider the majority of your conversations with friends. Do they show evidence of the Spirit's continuous filling?

7. What do singing and making music in your heart to the Lord express? (Ephesians 5:20) Does your heart reflect this mark of the Spirit?

8. "Always giving thanks to God the Father for everything" is one of the four mentioned characteristics of a Spirit-filled life (Ephesians 5:20). What are some attitudes or actions that would disqualify a person who claims to be Spirit filled?

9. In Ephesians 5:21ff, Christians are taught to submit to one another. Can you think of any examples from your own relationships which would prove or negate your being filled with the Spirit?

10. Read Acts 6:1-7; 11:19-24; and 13:52. What did these believers have in common? How did their lives give credit to this condition? Was this a special condition for a select few or was it intended to be enjoyed by all Christians? Support your answer from the text.

11. Read the following passages and determine when and for what purpose these Christians were filled with the Holy Spirit.

   Acts 4:8ff

   Acts 4:31

   Acts 7:55ff

   Acts 13:9-12

12. Does your life show evidence of being continually Spirit-filled? Why or why not? If not, what should you do to ensure it does?

For Further Study
   1. Read John Stott's *Baptism and Fullness* (InterVarsity). Write a one-page explanation of the difference between the initial experience of being indwelt by the Spirit at conversion and the continuous experience of being filled with the Spirit.
   2. Review each Digging Deeper section and write a summary of what you have learned about the Holy Spirit for each. Share your results with your small group or pastor.

•TOOL CHEST•
(A Suggested Optional Resource)

BAPTISM AND FULLNESS
John R.W. Stott's *Baptism and Fullness* (InterVarsity) is a small and succinct treatise on the work of the Holy Spirit. Stott develops four categories: The Promise of the Spirit, the Fullness of the Spirit, the Fruit of the Spirit, and the Gifts of the Spirit. If you struggle with deep questions about the nature of the baptism of the Spirit, "the second blessing," or other topics related to the Spirit's activity, Stott's work is worth consulting.